the gospel course

by Brian Clark

LIVING
FAITH
BOOKS

lffellowship.com

brianclark.org

But these are written, that ye might believe that Jesus is the Christ, the Son of God; and that believing ye might have life through his name.

John 20:31

Living Faith Books
3953 Walnut St
Kansas City, MO 64111

Cover Design: Brandon Briscoe
Formatting: Joel Springer
Editor: Melissa Wharton
ISBN: 978-1-950004-04-1
Printed in the United States of America

contents

preface

Why is a course like this necessary? And why is it that Christians across the planet are engaged in a single mission to share the gospel with each and every person?

The reason is God. This world and all that is in it was created with one ultimate purpose: we were created for his glory, his honour, and his pleasure. The glory of God is truth, perfect holiness, and everlasting love, and we exist to receive his glory, reflect it onto others, and return it back to him in thanksgiving and praise. That is why we share the gospel: to show the greatness of God. Satan seeks to blind everyone from the light of God's glorious gospel. That is why we must preach Christ in all the world among whom we shine as lights in the darkness.

Our love for God and our pursuit for his glory is what drives us to share the gospel, and is the main purpose for this little booklet. We strive to see God glorified and worshiped as he should be. We want to see people saved and enjoy the benefits that come with salvation, but God's glory is the ultimate reason why the gospel must be preached throughout the world.

There is also a very practical purpose for this course. It was written in response to a very practical need. Many believers have the desire to share their faith, to share the gospel of Jesus Christ with others. But at the same time we live in a day when statistics claim that most Christians never share Christ with someone else. Why is that? There could be many reasons. It could be fear, which we all understand too well. But there is another reason that stops many from taking the step to share. I believe that most Christians want to share Christ with others, but they simply don't know what to say. As believers, they know the gospel and they believe the gospel. They certainly know it well enough to place their own faith in it. They learn about it every week and sing about it every Sunday. Yes, they know the gospel. However, knowing the gospel and explaining the gospel are two very different things. To lay the gospel out in a biblical way that is both comprehensive and easy to understand would be a challenge for anyone.

The Gospel Course was written to help answer that need. This booklet is meant both to explain the gospel to those who do not yet know Christ and to be an encouragement to believers. I want all Christians to have the confidence that, when the opportunity arises, they not only have the desire to share the gospel but the words as well.

introduction

This is a faithful saying, and worthy of all acceptation, that Christ Jesus came into the world to save sinners; of whom I am chief.

1 Timothy 1:15

"This is a faithful saying."

That is another way of saying that this is true. Unlike most things you see on a screen, what you are about to hear is a true story. It is not a movie story. It is more like a news story that affects us all. And this news story is "worthy of all acceptation." That means you should believe it. Urgent news is of no use unless it is believed. So here is the true and urgent news I would like to share.

"Christ Jesus came into the world to save sinners." If this story was posted on a news site, that would be the headline. It also gives us the three parts into which this booklet is divided: The Sin of Man, The Salvation of God, and the Saviour of the World. Each lesson is then divided into two sections: The Scriptures and The Story. The scriptures teach the truth of the gospel, while the story brings it to life practically. This course can be used one-on-one for personal evangelism, as well as in a small group setting as part of a church's corporate outreach.

1 Timothy 1:15 ends with the phrase, "Of whom I am chief." That means the person sharing this is a sinner just like us; in fact, they may be worse. But the Bible reveals how we all can be righteous before God. The good news of Jesus Christ is true, and if it is believed it will change the course of your life forever.

the sins of man

the scriptures

Every one of them is gone back: they are altogether become filthy; there is none that doeth good, no, not one.

Psalm 53:3

Our Spirit is Dead - broken branches

Our sin has separated us from God, like a tree branch broken off and separated from its source of life. It looks the same for a while, but in time it will wither and die.

Genesis 2:16–17
Isaiah 59:2
Ephesians 2:1-2

Our Heart is Dark - barren branches

We are born with a sin nature. No one has to teach a child to lie or disobey. Even when we do right, it is not for God's glory but for man's. As broken branches cannot produce fruit, so we cannot serve God in righteousness as we were intended.

Genesis 6:5
Romans 1:21
John 3:19

Our Soul is Damned - burning branches

The only thing left to do with dead branches is to gather them up and throw them in the fire to be burned. This is the destiny of all who will not obey the gospel.

Mark 16:16
Matthew 13:41-42
Luke 12:5
2 Thessalonians 1:7-9

These are the scriptures. Now let's turn to the story so we can see what this looks like.

the story

The Story of the Runaway & the Rule Keeper

Luke 15:11-32

Jesus tells the story about a man with two sons. One ran from his father to enjoy sin. The other son stayed home and kept the rules. By this, Jesus reveals two kinds of sinners. There are The Runaways and The Rule-keepers: two different approaches, but the same heart. One is the sin of self-indulgence. The other, the sin of self-righteousness.

Consider this. If you could have one thing that would make you feel secure or make you feel like somebody, what would it be? The problem with mankind is that the answer to this question is never God.
We are all the sons in this story. We all want the good life, and we want to be viewed as a good person. We endeavour to achieve this in two ways. The irreligious run from God to get it, taking pleasure in their sin while pretending God is not there. The religious use God to get it, taking pride in their "righteousness" while pretending their sin isn't there.

The Bible teaches that whether you are a good citizen or a crook, religious or atheist, priest or prostitute, we are all guilty of sin against God and are condemned to everlasting fire in hell. We all love sin more than we love God.

But thankfully, that is not the end of the story.

notes

the salvation of God

the scriptures

For this is good and acceptable in the sight of God our Saviour; Who will have all men to be saved ...

1 Timothy 2:3-4

Salvation is being rescued by God - forgiven

God wants to rescue us from eternal damnation and reconcile us back to himself, declaring us righteous, making us his children, and giving us eternal life. As with the runaway who hated his father, a good father only wants for his child to return safe and sound.

Psalm 86:5
Romans 4:6
Galatians 4:4-6
Romans 6:23

Salvation is received by grace - for free

God is waiting for us with nothing but grace. Salvation is granted to us not because of our good deeds, but freely because of his mercy. Like a runaway who returns, he does not earn his way back. A good father accepts him freely as his son.

Ephesians 2:8–9
Titus 3:5

Salvation is reserved in glory - forever

God promises a home in heaven. Salvation is a promise that one day we will go home to be with our Father forever. Like a runaway who is reconciled, a good father will take him home.

Ephesians 1:13
John 14:2-3
Revelation 21:4

These are the scriptures. Now let's turn to our story so we can see what this looks like.

the story

The Rest of the Story

Luke 15:11-32

The runaway son finally comes to his senses and decides to return to his father. He devises a plan to work off the money he took so that he could earn his way back into his father's good graces.

He arrives to find his father waiting and watching for his return. His father runs to him and embraces and kisses him. And before the lost son could pitch his own plan of redemption, the father called for a new robe for his son, a ring for his finger, and shoes for his feet. The robe represents the righteousness that God gives to us, the ring represents our sonship, and the shoes represent the newness of life we can now walk in. This story pictures what awaits every runaway who returns.

The father rejoiced that his son was lost but now he is found, he was dead but now he is alive. Then he brought his son home where a great feast was waiting, picturing not only the joy we have now, but the home that awaits us in heaven.

The elder brother, however, remained outside. The father went to him and invited him in, but Jesus does not tell us what he finally decided. That is because the choice is yours. You are standing outside and God is inviting you in. What will you choose?

Now there's only one more thing you need to know.

notes

the saviour
of the
world

the scriptures

And we have seen and do testify that the Father sent the Son to be the Saviour of the world.

1 John 4:14

Jesus Christ is the Son of God

God is three in one: Father, Son, Holy Spirit. Jesus Christ is God the Son. God the Father sent his Son to be the saviour of the world.

1 John 5:20
Mark 14:61-62
Philippians 2:5-8
John 3:16

Jesus Christ is the Sacrifice for Sin

God sent his Son to die as a sacrifice for sin, in our place as our substitute. Jesus died on the cross and rose again to purchase our salvation.

1 John 4:10
2 Corinthians 5:21
1 Corinthians 15:3-4
Romans 5:8

Jesus Christ is Standing at the Door

Receiving the salvation of God is not complicated. It's like a friend who is knocking at the door; all you have to do is open up and let him in.

Revelation 3:20
Isaiah 45:22
Matthew 11:28

These are the scriptures. Now let's turn to our story so we can see what this looks like.

the story

The Mystery in the Story

Luke 15:11-32

There's something so easy to overlook when you read this story. We see two sons who are lost, and we see the happiness of the father when his lost son returns and is reconciled. But there is an important truth hidden in the story. In films they call it an easter egg, which in this case is quite a coincidence. Before they can go home to eat and be merry, the father commands his servants to bring the fatted calf and kill it (vs. 23). This is a picture of Christ and his death on the cross hidden within the story.

We are all sinners, and God the Father desires to save us from our sin and bring us home. But before he can do that, there is the need for a saviour. A sacrifice must be made to pay the penalty for sin so that God can forgive us, for free, forever.

That is what Jesus Christ did. He chose to lay down his life as a sacrifice to God, in our place, to pay the price for our sins. He is the one who makes it possible for all the runaways and rule-keepers to come home, where our Father waits for us with open arms of mercy and grace. He is waiting to clothe us with righteousness, place a ring on our finger signifying that we are his sons, and put new shoes on our feet to walk in eternal life with him. With his grace comes a promise that we will soon go home to be with him in heaven, forever.

Just like the elder brother deciding if he would join his father inside or remain in his pride, the choice is now yours.

notes

What Do I Do Now?

In the story, all the elder brother had to do was receive his father's invitation and come inside. Like the elder brother, we all stand at the same crossroads. We all have a choice to make.

What Does That Mean?

Standing at the crossroads means you have to choose which way you will turn. What is often called "getting saved" or "becoming a Christian" is what the Bible calls repentance. This word simply means to turn; in the Bible, it means to turn from your sin to God. This involves two things.

1 Believe in Jesus Christ

Salvation is by faith alone. All you have to do is believe in Christ's sacrifice for your sin.

Romans 4:5
But to him that worketh not, but believeth on him that justifieth the ungodly, his faith is counted for righteousness.

Romans 10:9
That if thou shalt confess with thy mouth the Lord Jesus, and shalt believe in thine heart that God hath raised him from the dead, thou shalt be saved.

2 Receive Jesus Christ

Salvation is a gift, and all you have to do is take it. Simply pray to God and tell him that you know you are a sinner, that you believe in Christ Jesus, and that you want to receive his gift of salvation.

John 1:12
But as many as received him, to them gave he power to become the sons of God, even to them that believe on his name:

Romans 10:13
For whosoever shall call upon the name of the Lord shall be saved.

Discussion: Which brother are you?

notes

www.ingramcontent.com/pod-product-compliance
Lightning Source LLC
Chambersburg PA
CBHW060550030426
42337CB00021B/4515